Instructions

1
Cut out the model of the house following the continuous outer line marked in black.

2
Fold the model of the house in the areas that are marked with the dashed line.

3
Put glue on the areas that are marked with a gray area.

4
Assemble the parts of the house, joining the areas with glue.

You did it!
Your new little house is now ready, enjoy your work!

Use your imagination and have fun with your new little houses!

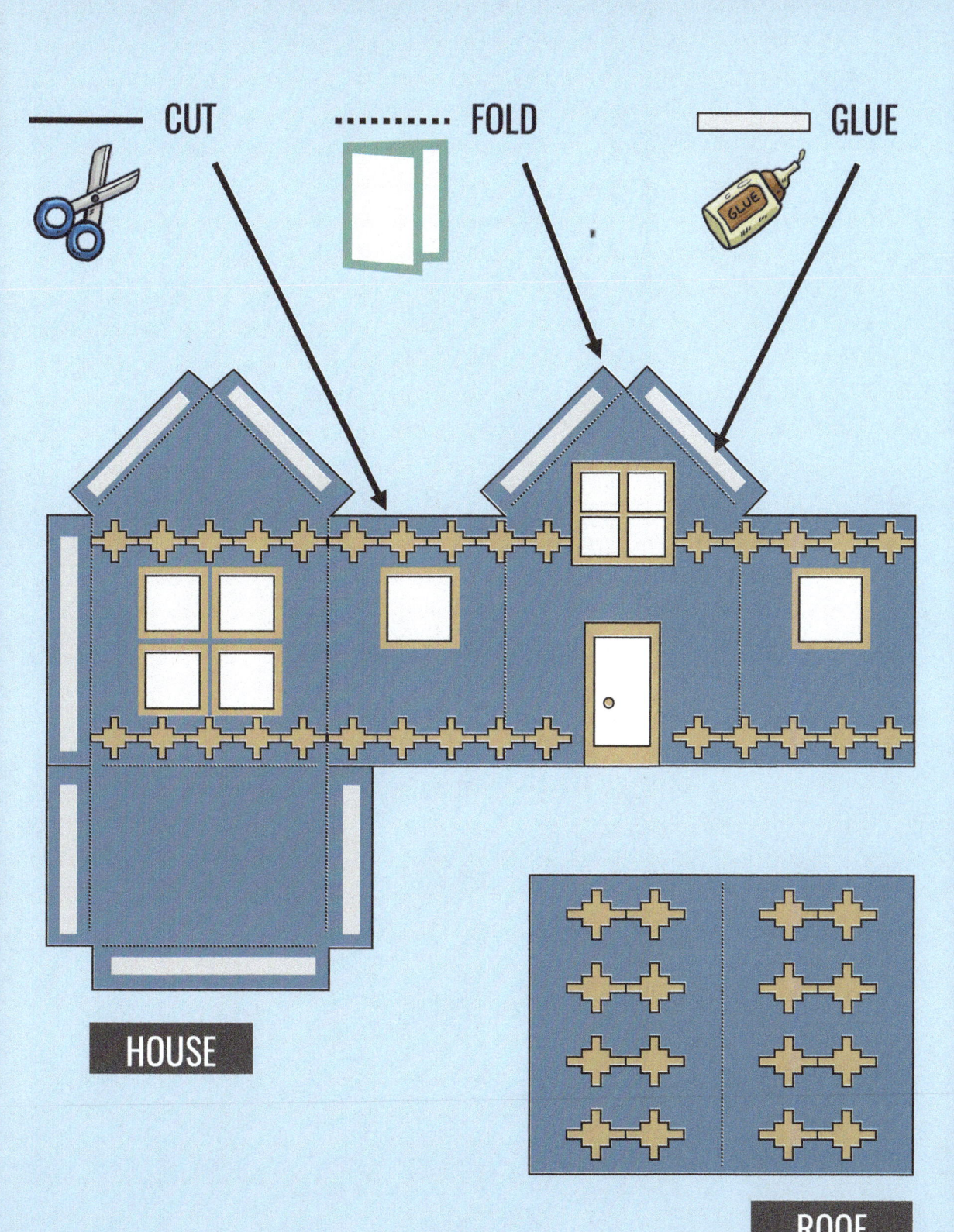

CUT ·········· FOLD GLUE

HOUSE

ROOF

PART
1

EXAMPLE

RESULT

MODEL

HOUSE

ROOF

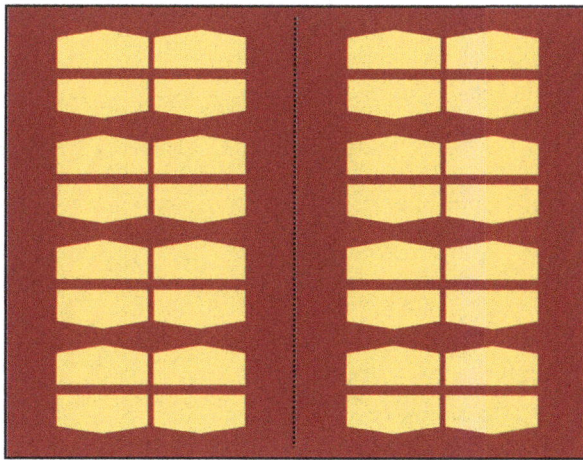

CUT

FOLD

GLUE

HOUSE

ROOF

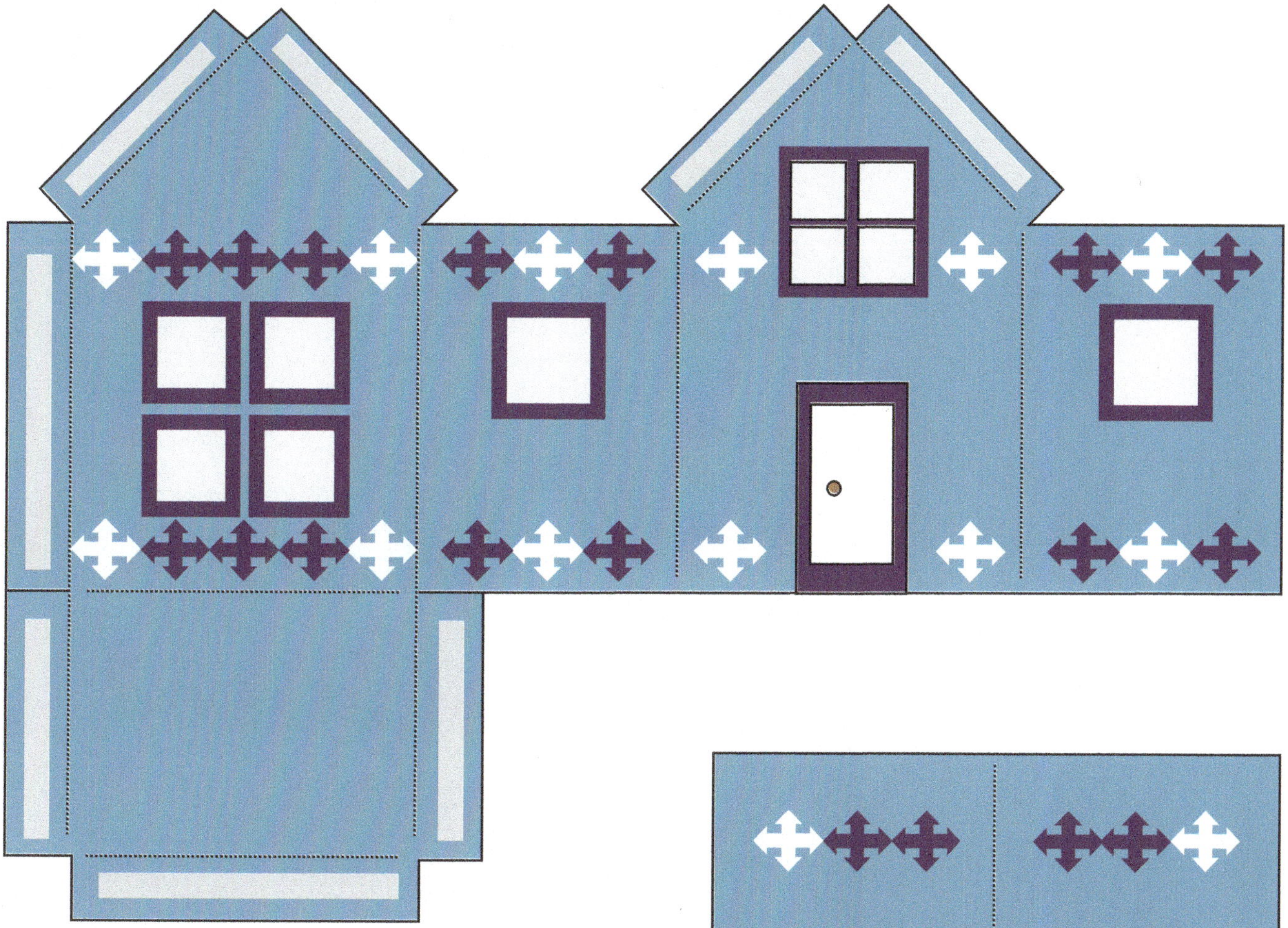

CUT

FOLD

GLUE

HOUSE

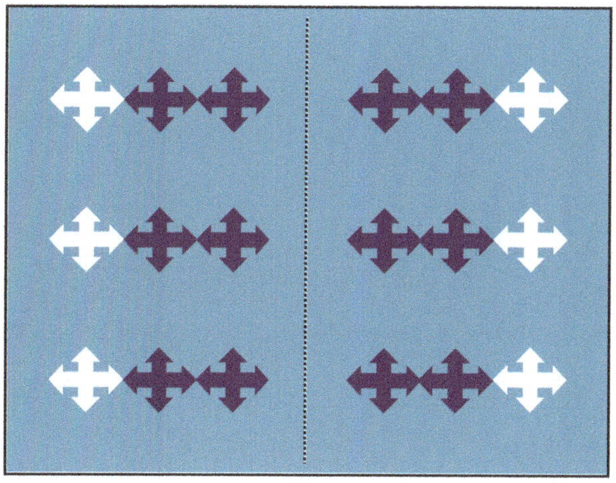

ROOF

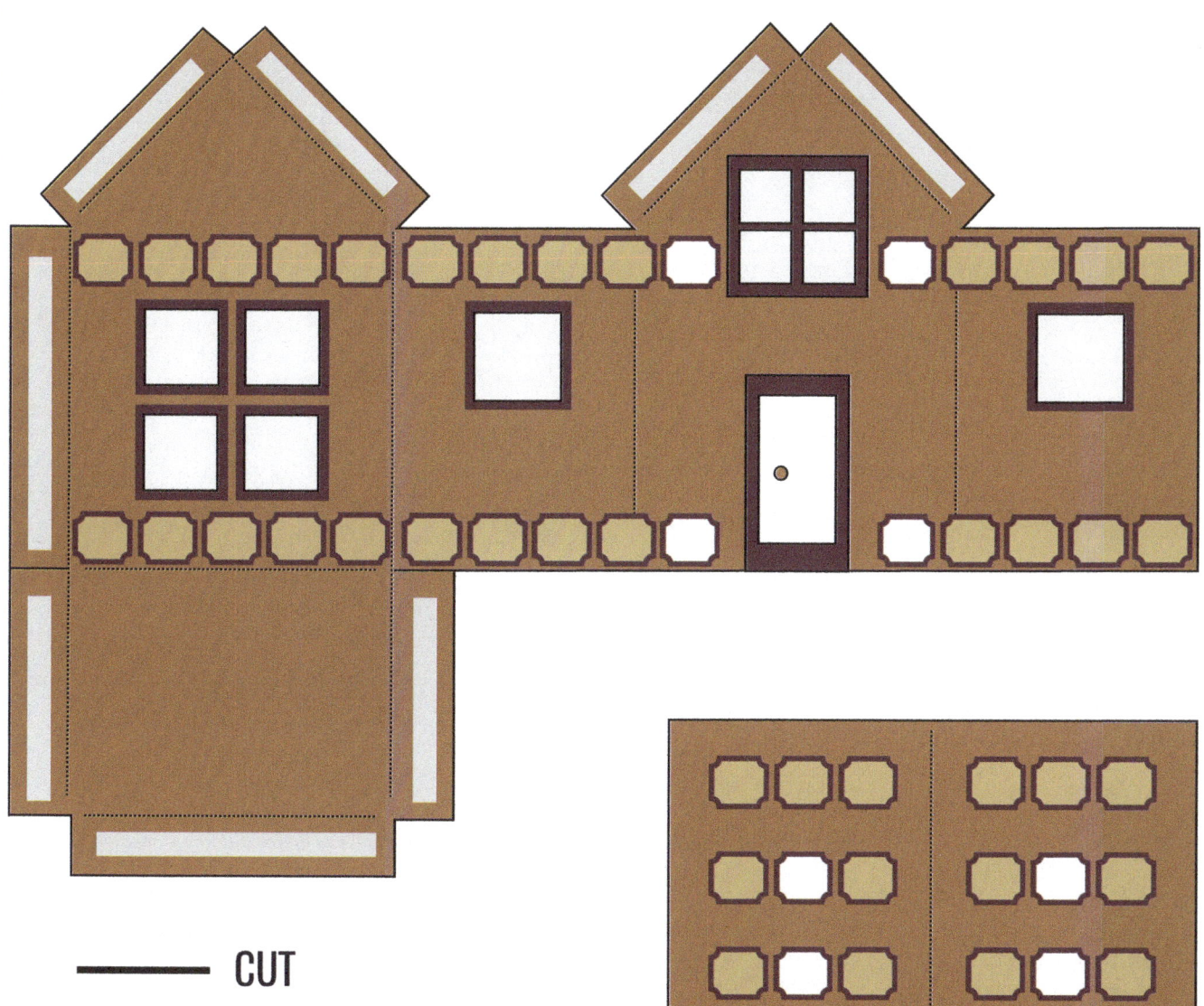

CUT

FOLD

GLUE

HOUSE

ROOF

CUT
FOLD
GLUE

HOUSE

ROOF

CUT
FOLD
GLUE

HOUSE

ROOF

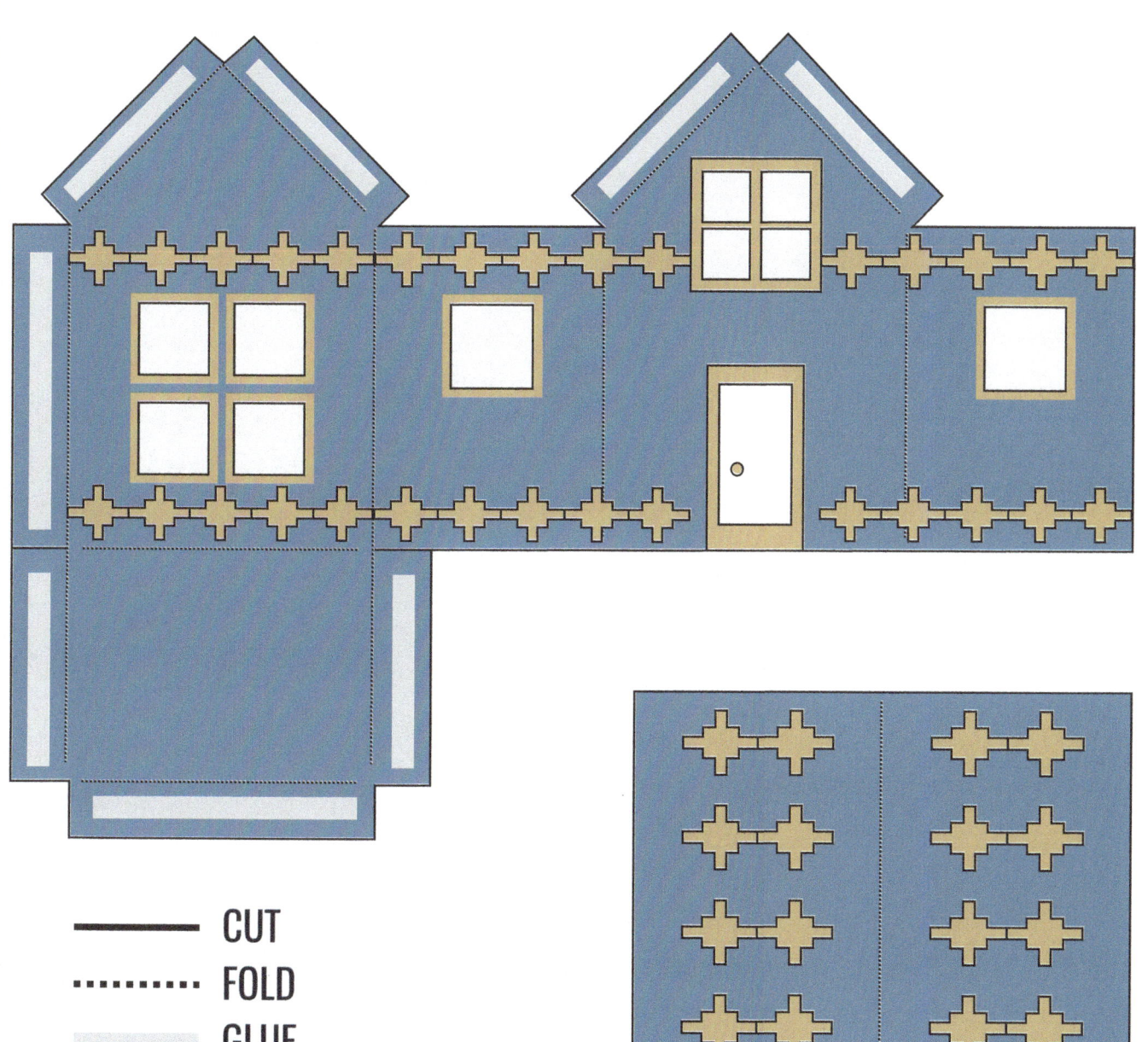

_____ CUT

.... FOLD

▬▬▬▬ GLUE

HOUSE

ROOF

PART
2

RESULT

MODEL

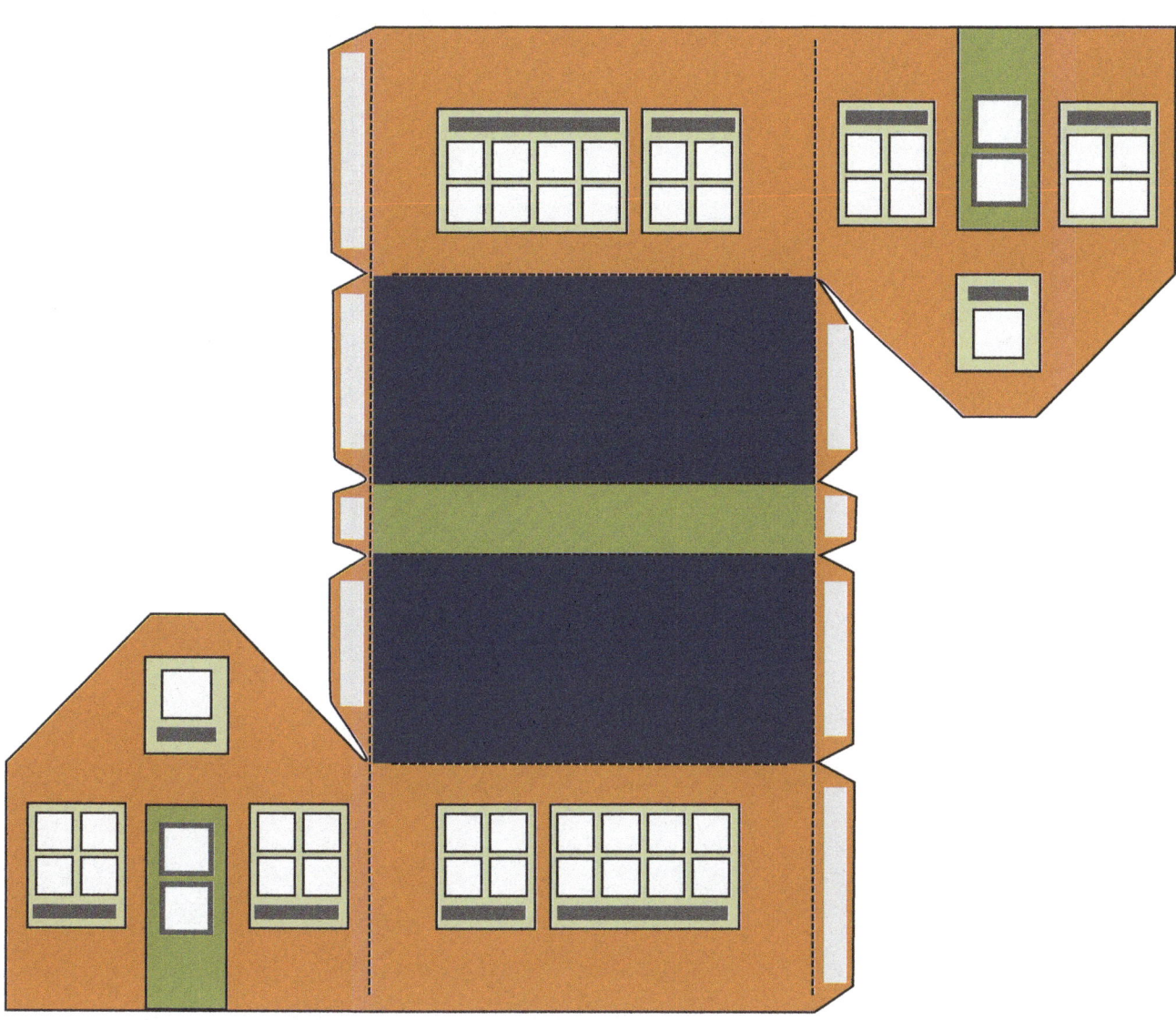

——————— CUT

·············· FOLD

░░░░░░░░ GLUE

HOUSE

CUT

FOLD

GLUE

HOUSE

HOUSE

——— CUT

·········· FOLD

GLUE

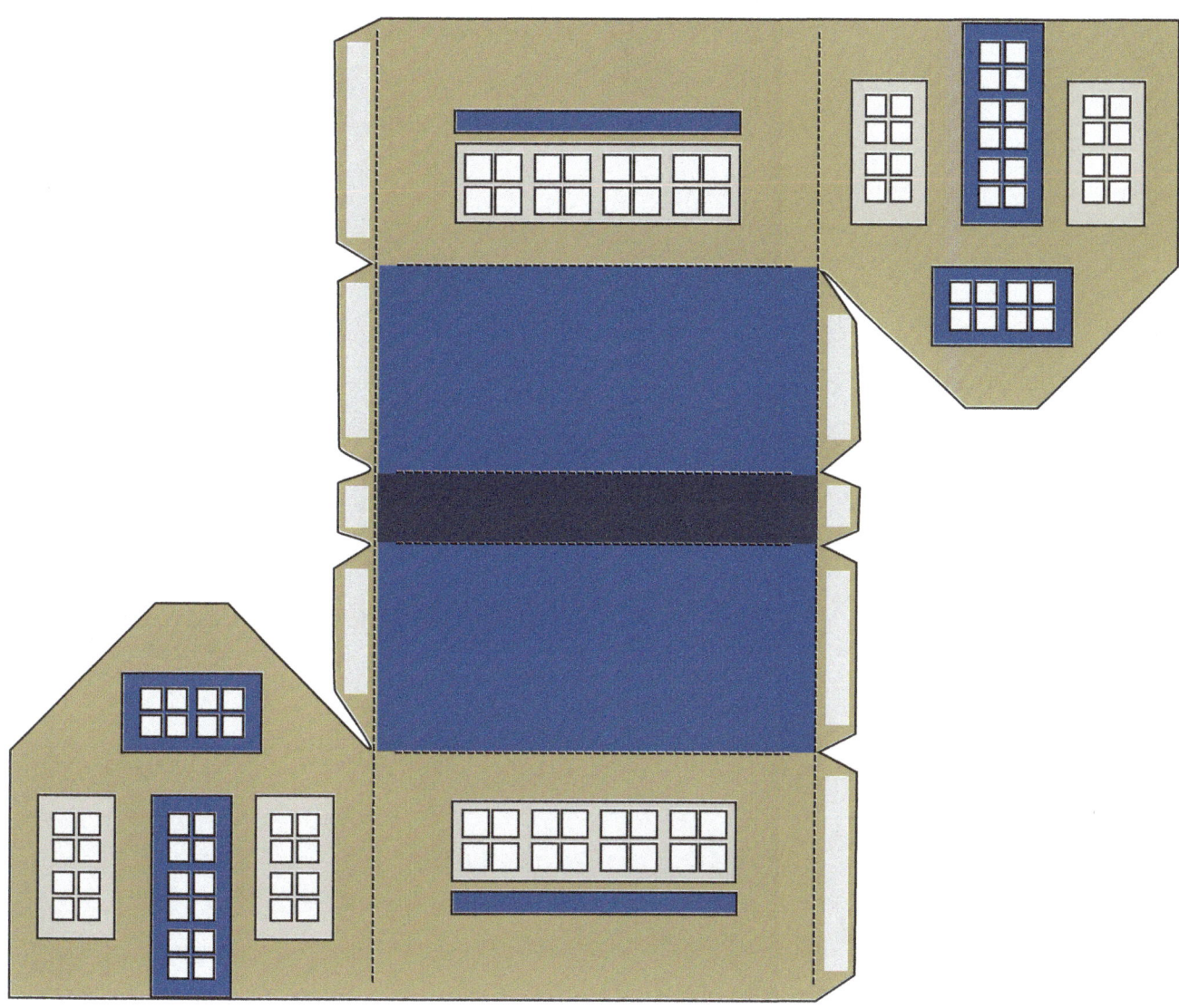

CUT
.... FOLD
GLUE

HOUSE

CUT

FOLD

GLUE

HOUSE

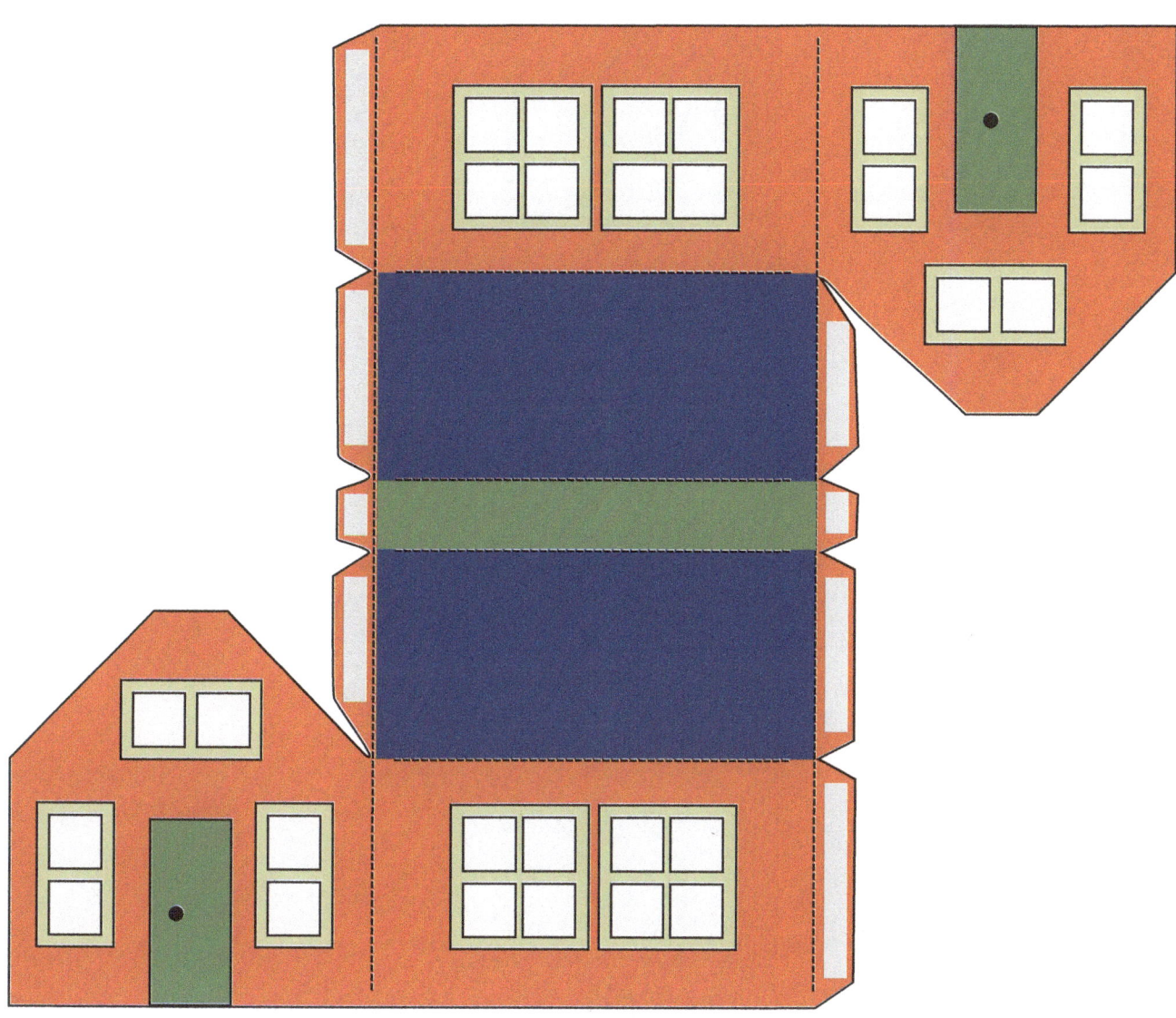

CUT
.... FOLD
GLUE

HOUSE

PART
3

EXAMPLE

RESULT

MODEL

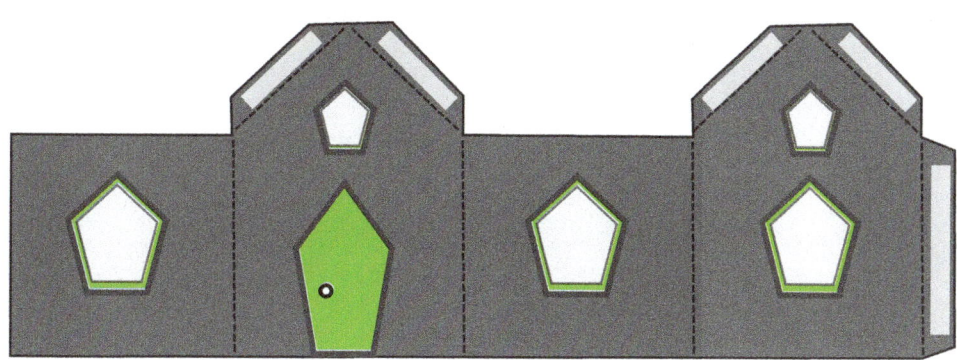

HOUSE

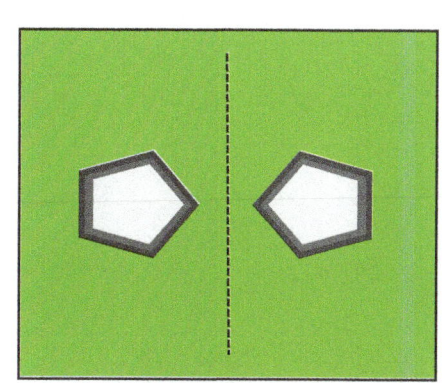

ROOF

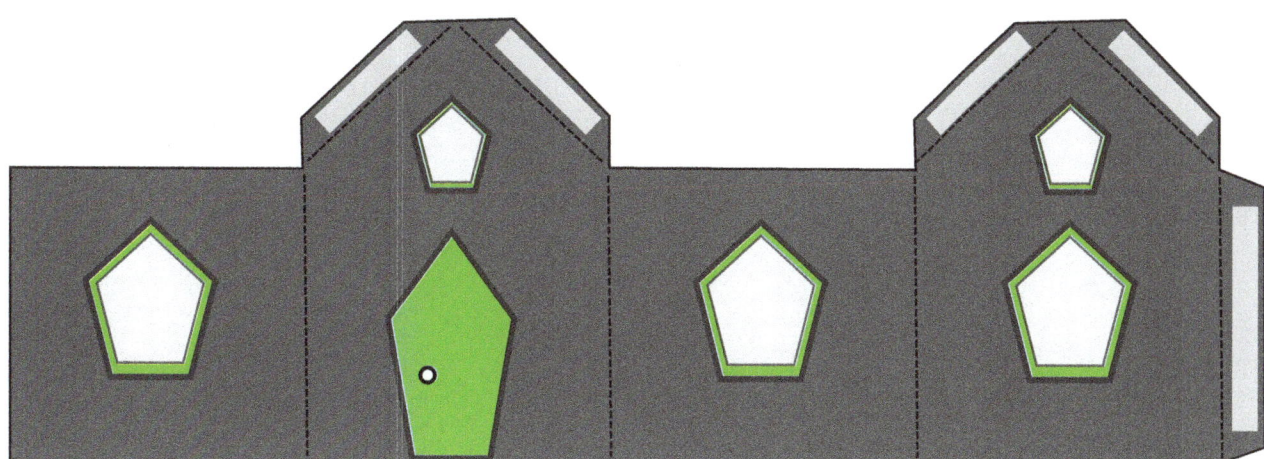

HOUSE

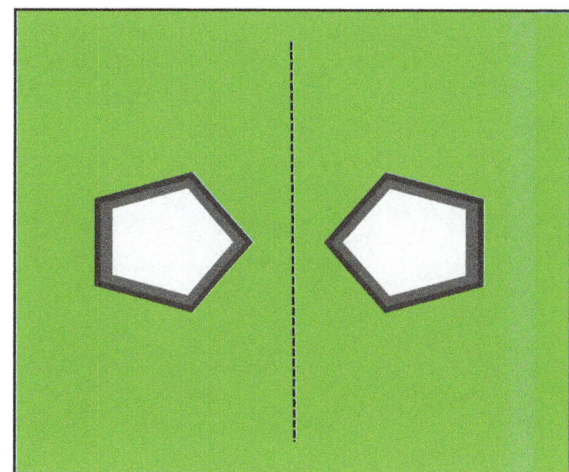

——————— CUT

············· FOLD

▬▬▬▬▬ GLUE

ROOF

HOUSE

—————— CUT

.... FOLD

—————— GLUE

ROOF

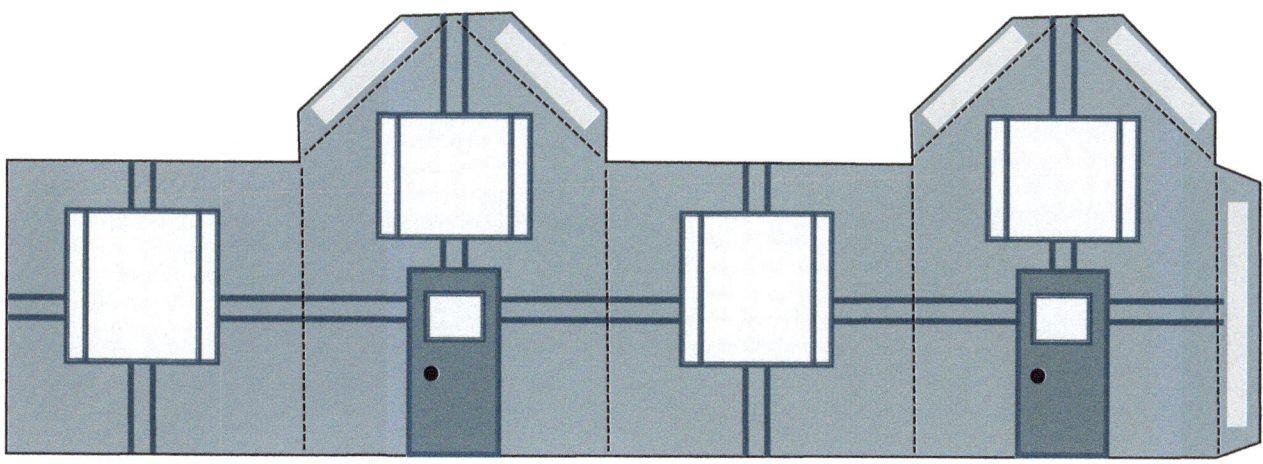

HOUSE

ROOF

—————— CUT

············ FOLD

—————— GLUE

HOUSE

———— CUT

·········· FOLD

▬▬▬▬ GLUE

ROOF

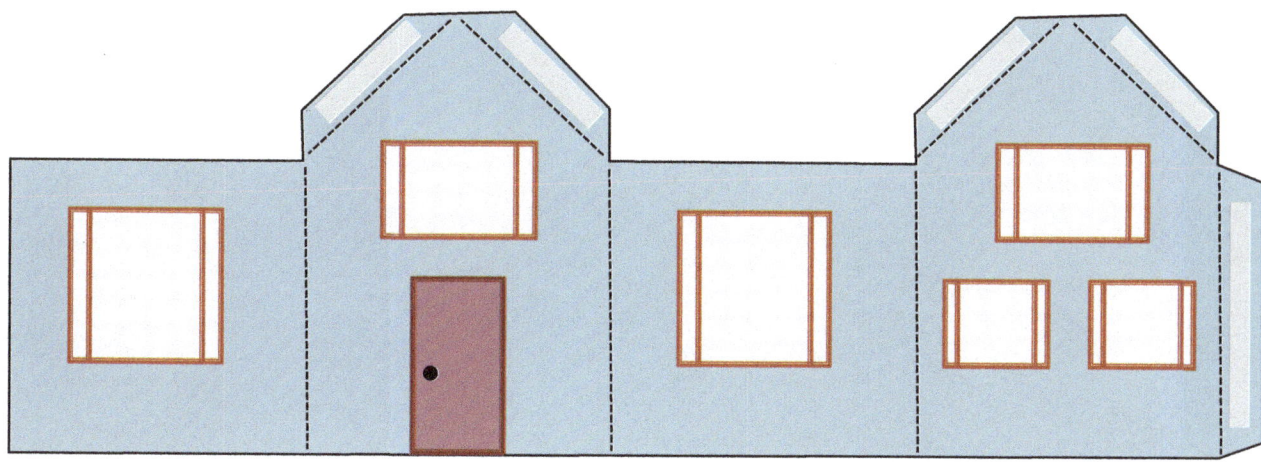

HOUSE

——————— CUT

············· FOLD

▬▬▬▬▬ GLUE

ROOF

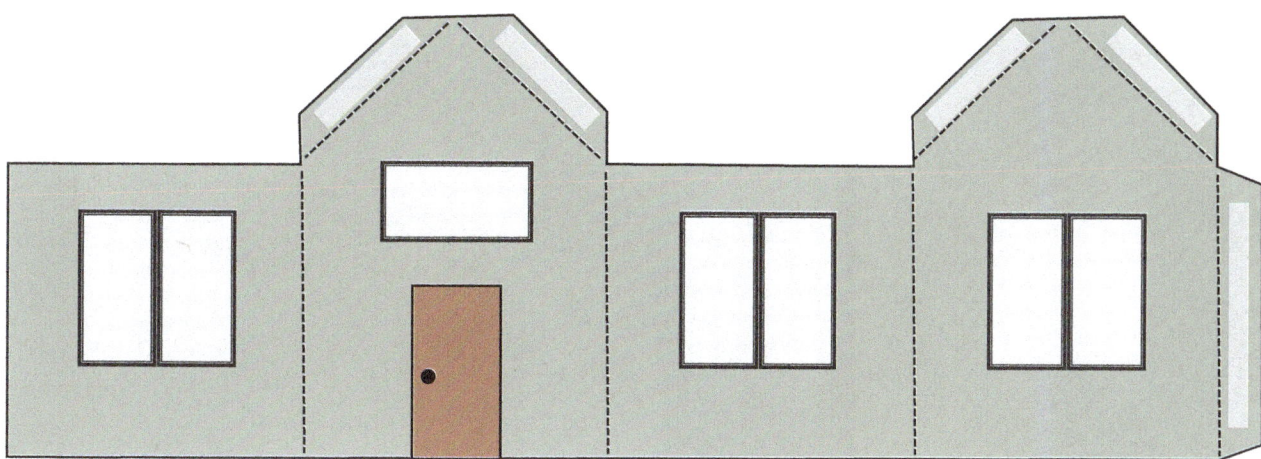

——————— CUT

··········· FOLD

▭▭▭▭▭▭ GLUE

PART
4

RESULT

MODEL

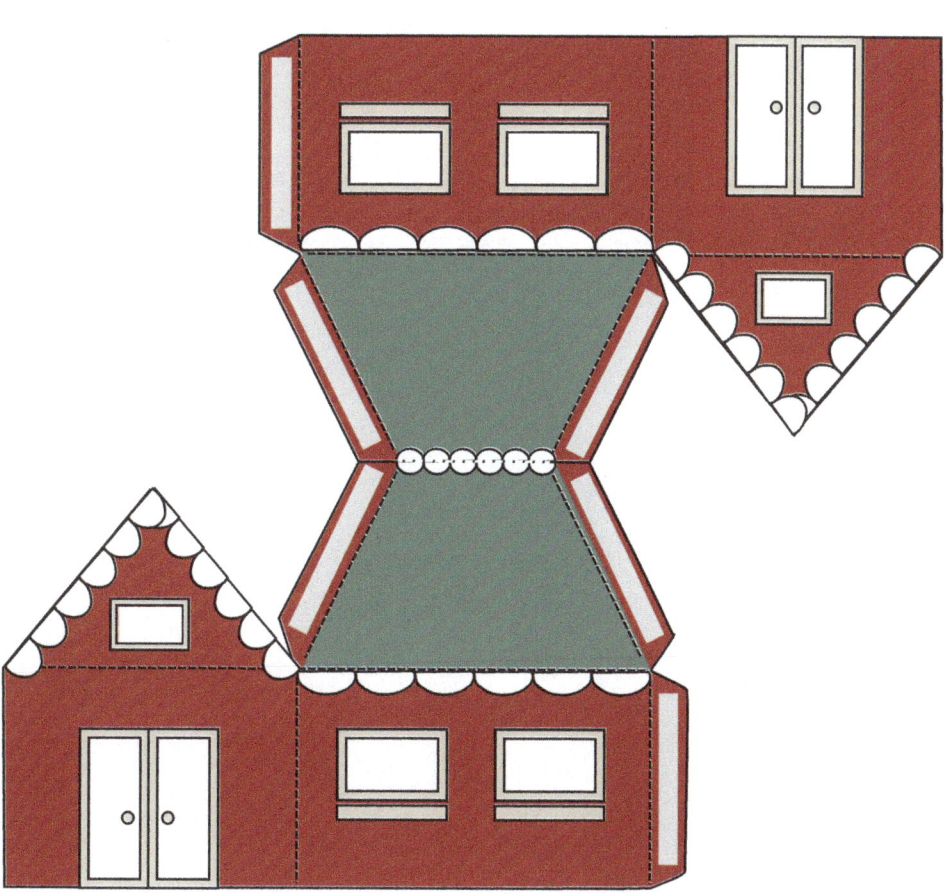

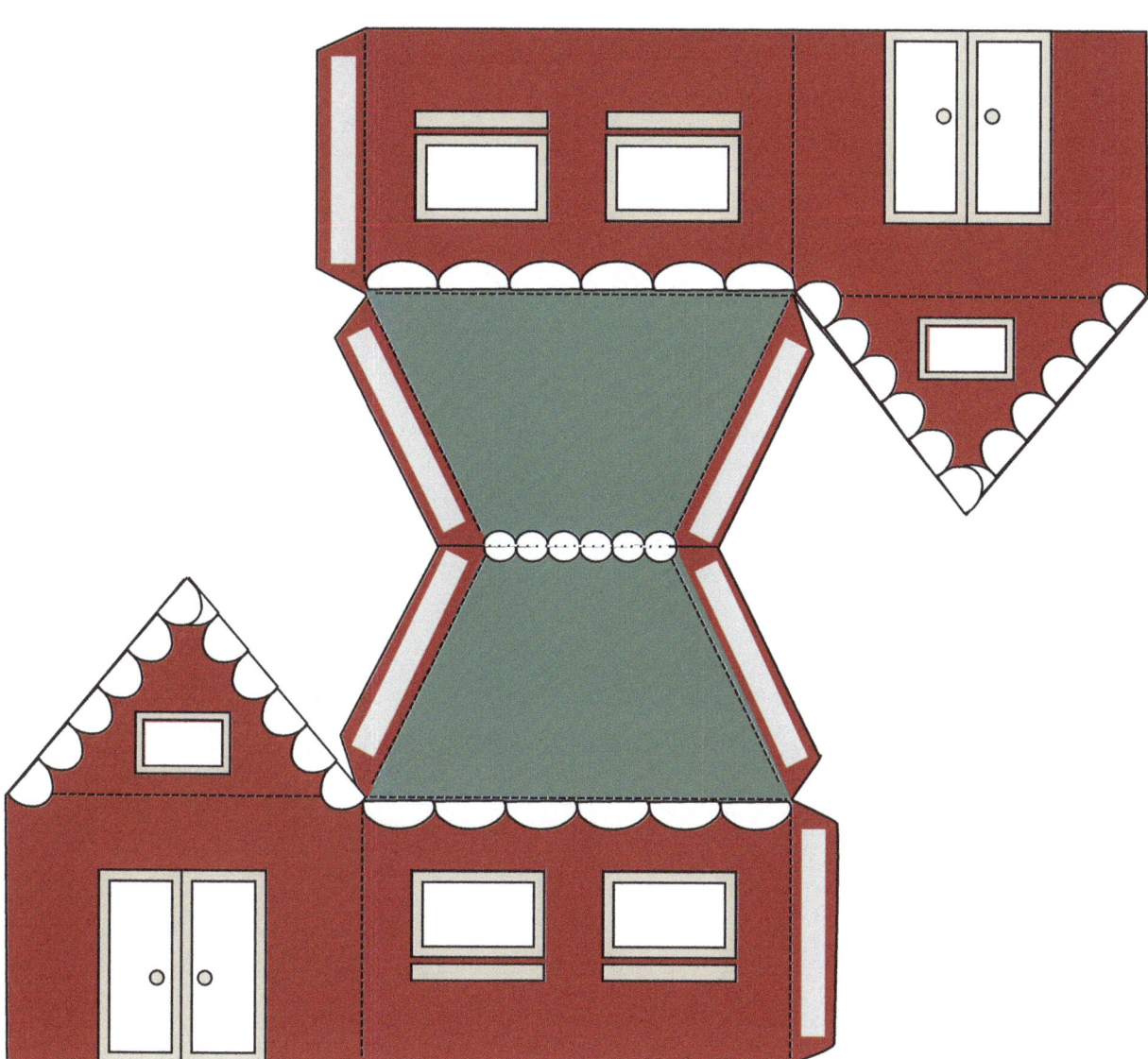

——————— CUT

············· FOLD

GLUE

HOUSE

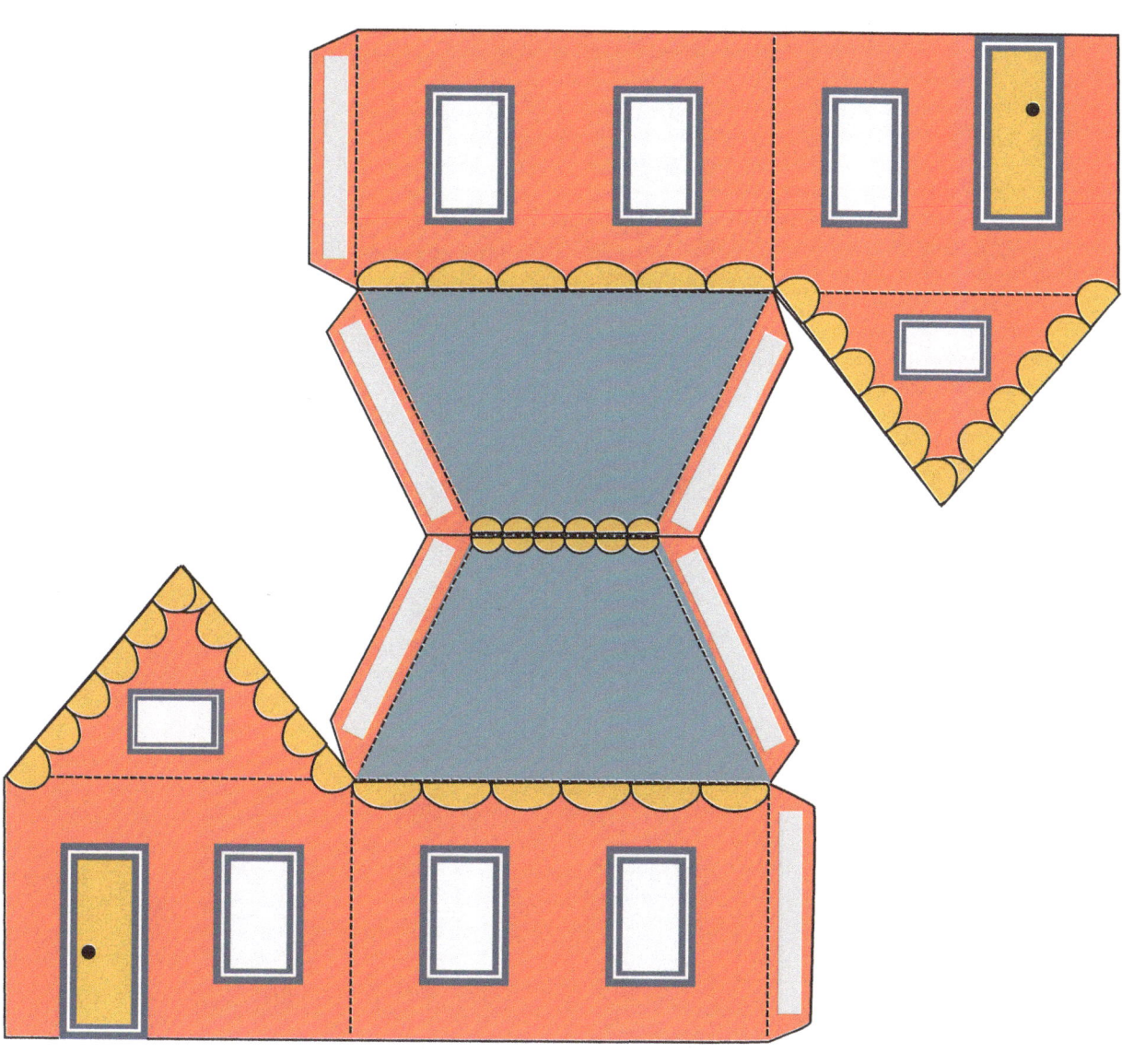

——————— CUT

············· FOLD

GLUE

HOUSE

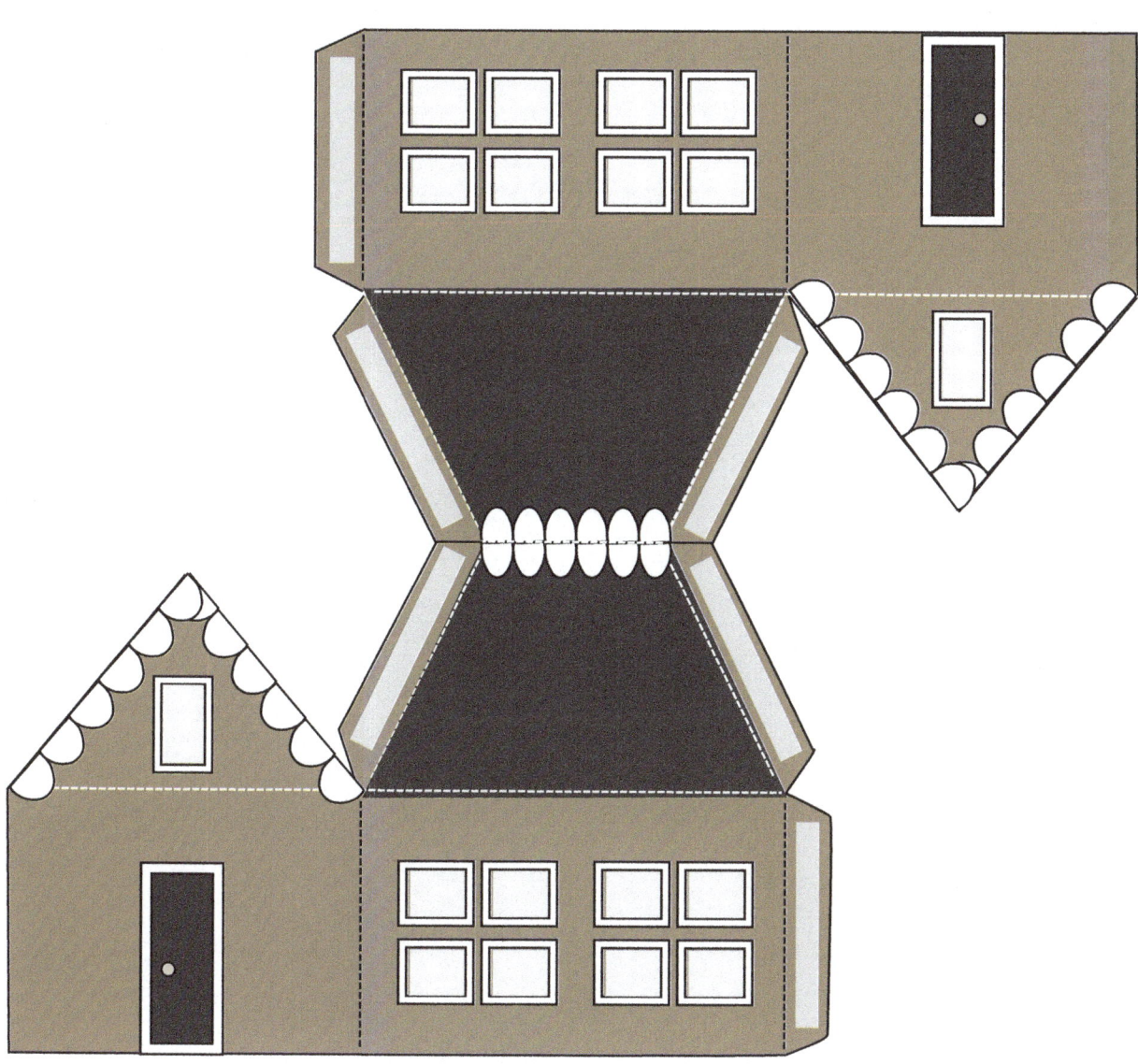

——————— CUT

·········· FOLD

▬▬▬▬▬▬ GLUE

HOUSE

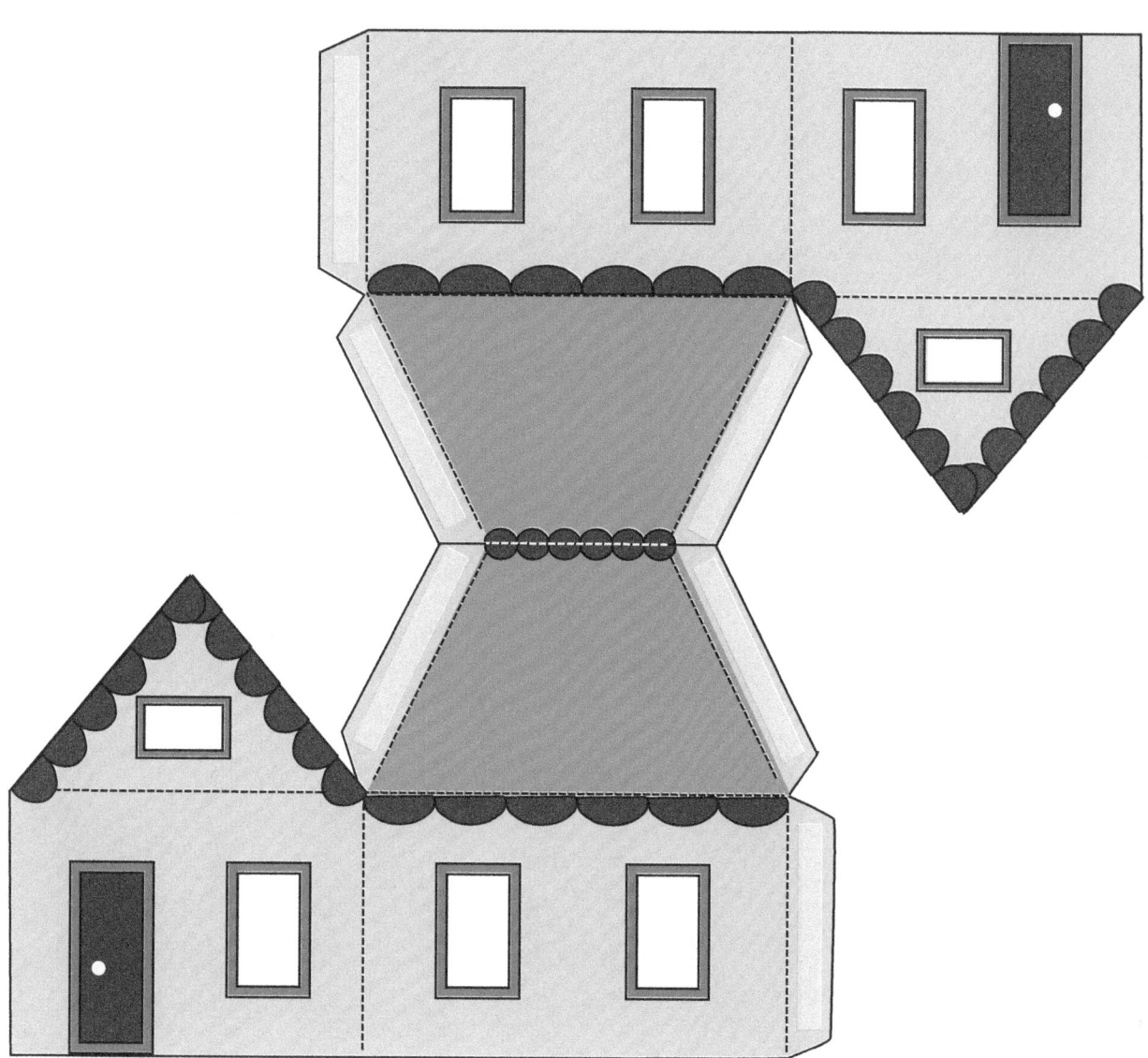

CUT

FOLD

GLUE

HOUSE

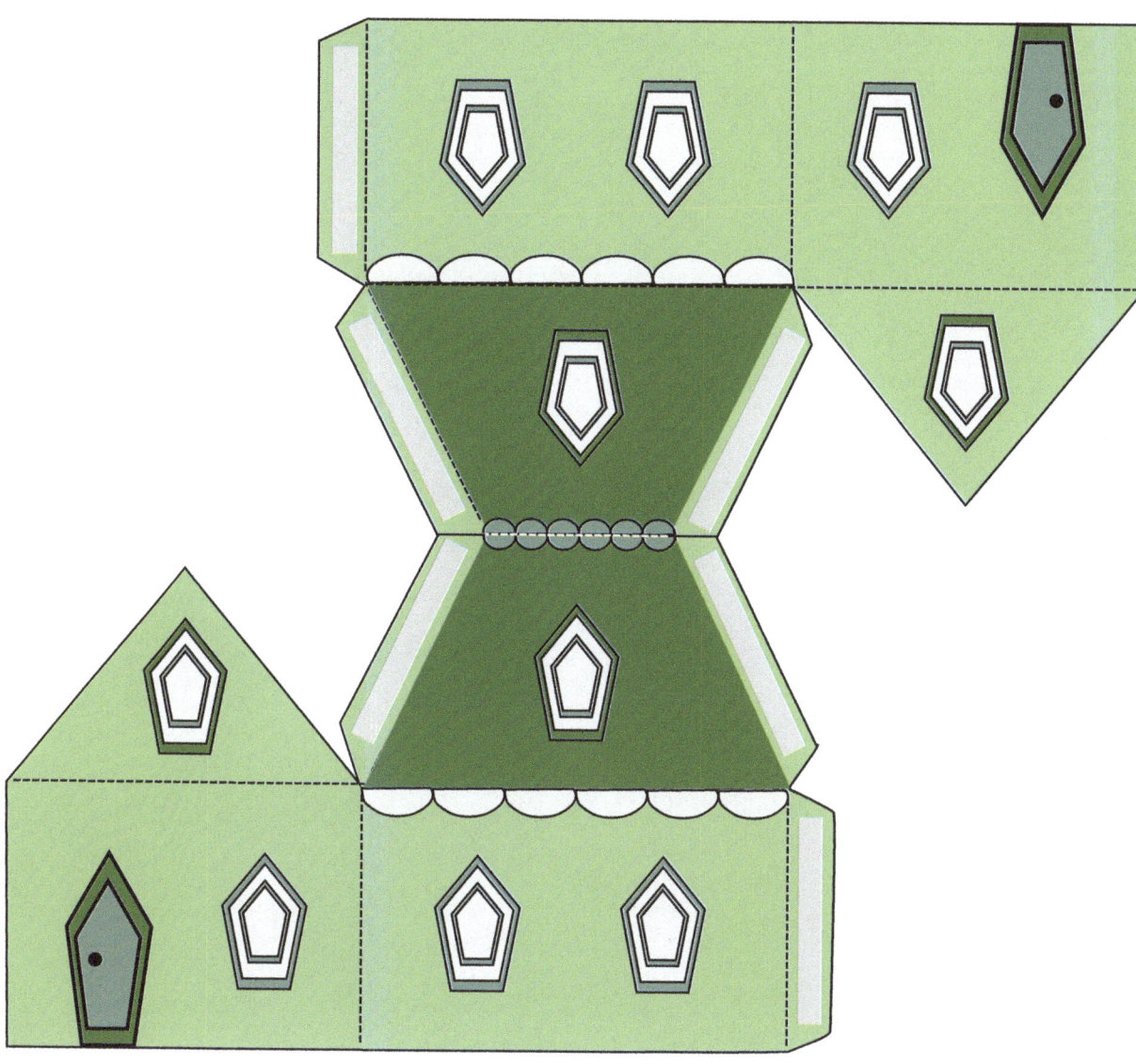

HOUSE

——————— CUT

·········· FOLD

GLUE

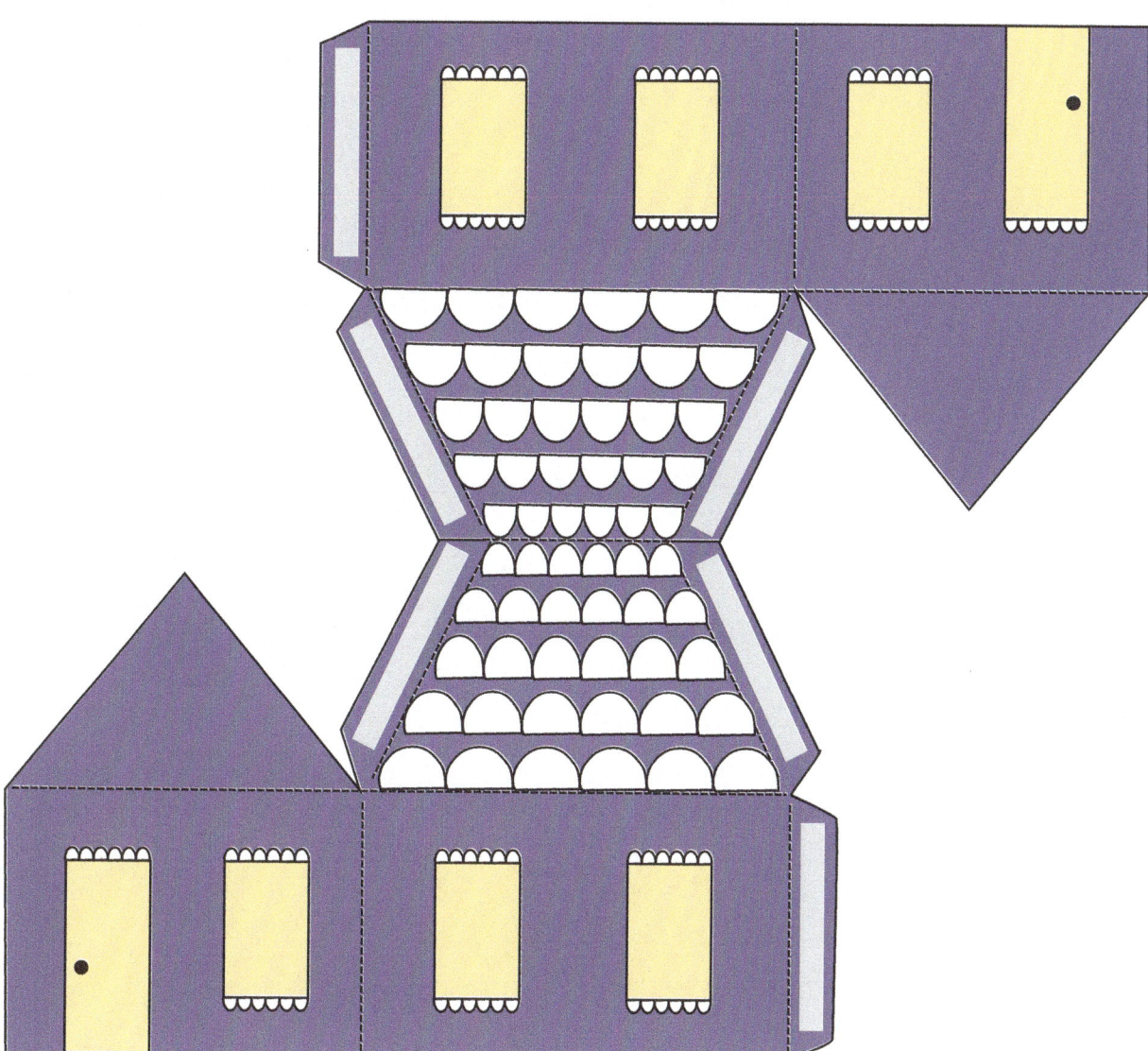

HOUSE

——————— CUT

············· FOLD

▬▬▬▬▬ GLUE

We have more books that you will love, check them online!

PAPER AIRPLANES

EASY TO MAKE PAPER AIRPLANES TO
CUT, ASSEMBLE AND PLAY!
Check the full series:
https://www.amazon.com/dp/B09FGPD7W6
https://www.amazon.co.uk/dp/B09FGPD7W6

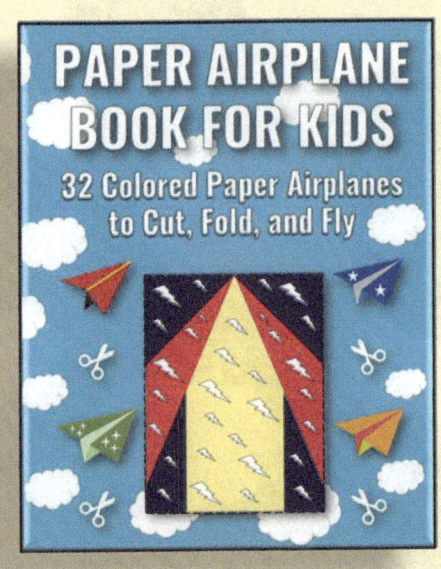

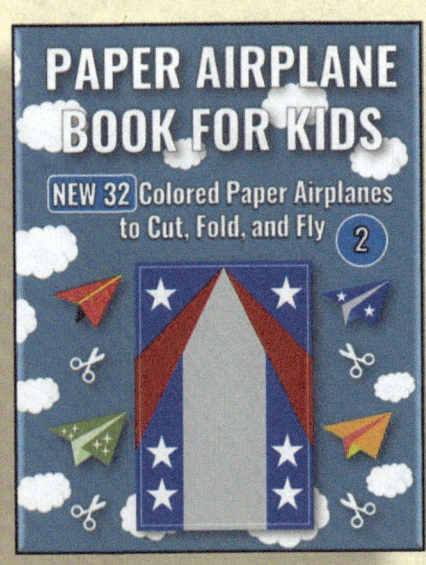

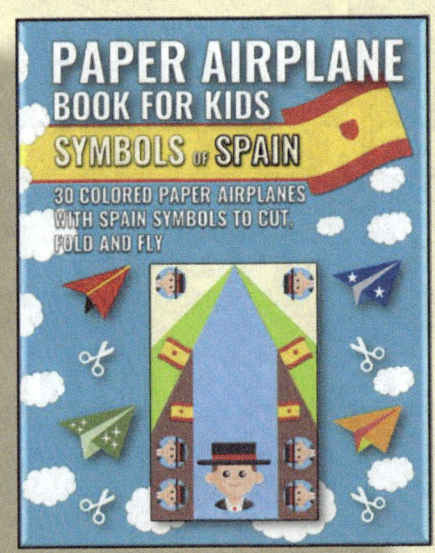

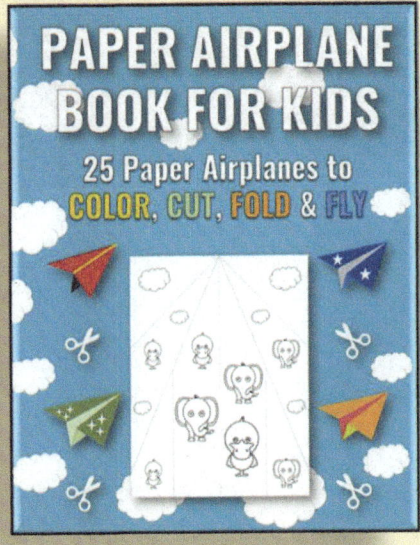

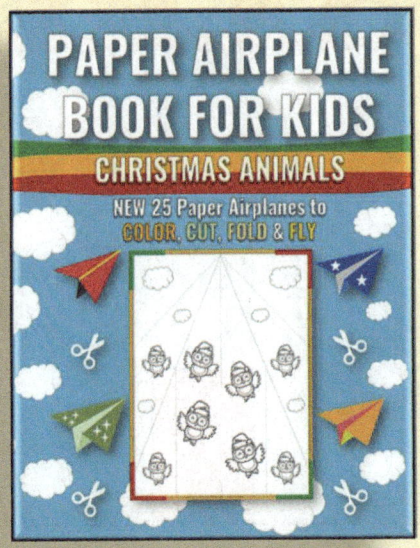

PAPER HOUSES

EASY TO MAKE PAPER MODELS TO CUT,
ASSEMBLE AND PLAY MANY TIMES!
Check the full series:
www.amazon.com/dp/B09QXTFVGP
www.amazon.co.uk/dp/B09QXTFVGP

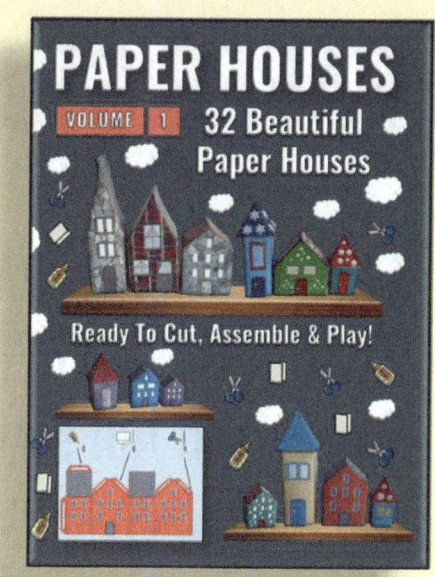

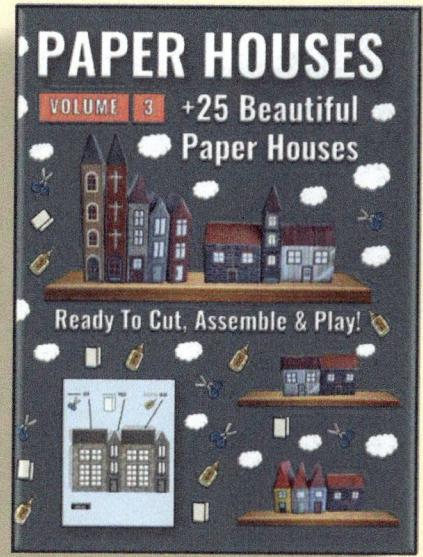

PAPER STORES

EASY TO MAKE PAPER MODELS TO CUT,
ASSEMBLE AND PLAY MANY TIMES!
Check the full series:
www.amazon.com/dp/B09XF8T279
www.amazon.co.uk/dp/B09XF8T279

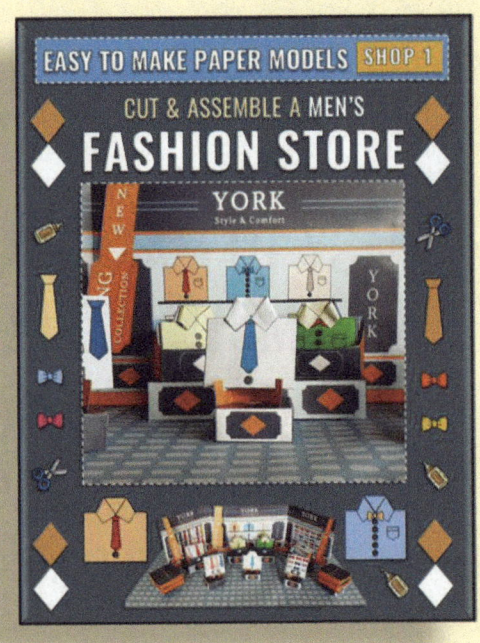

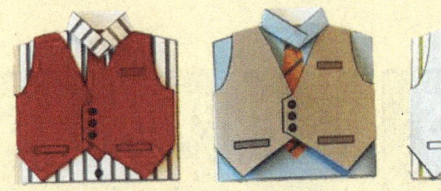

PAPER CARS

EASY TO MAKE PAPER CARS TO CUT, ASSEMBLE AND PLAY!
Check the full series:
https://www.amazon.com/dp/B0C5LB5QNB
https://www.amazon.co.uk/dp/B0C5LB5QNB

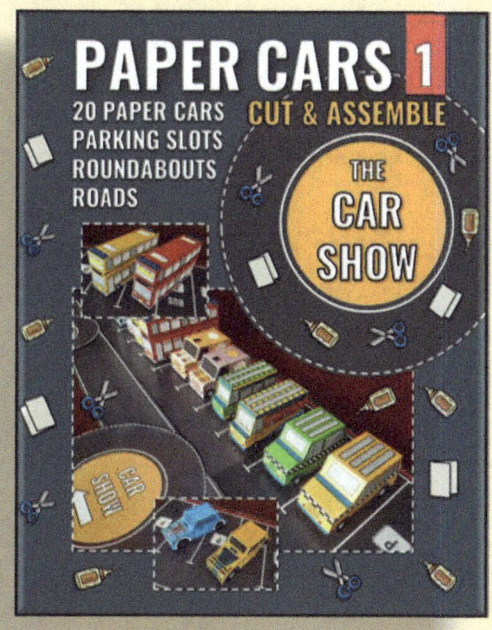

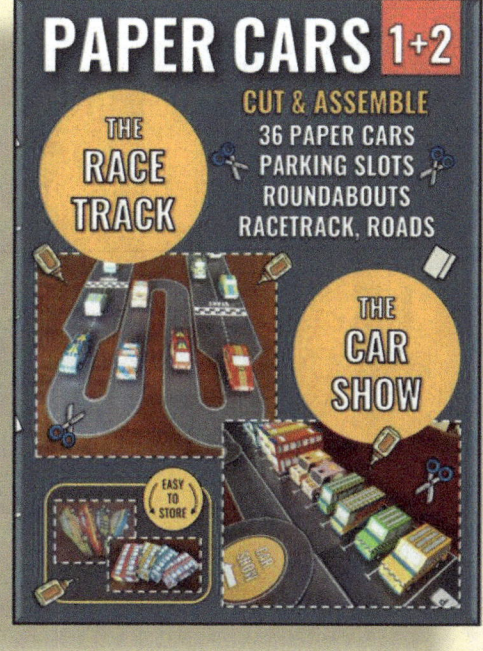

PAPER EXHIBITIONS

EASY TO MAKE PAPER MODELS TO CUT,
ASSEMBLE AND PLAY MANY TIMES!
Check the full series:
www.amazon.com/dp/B09VFSQWSX
www.amazon.co.uk/dp/B09VFSQWSX

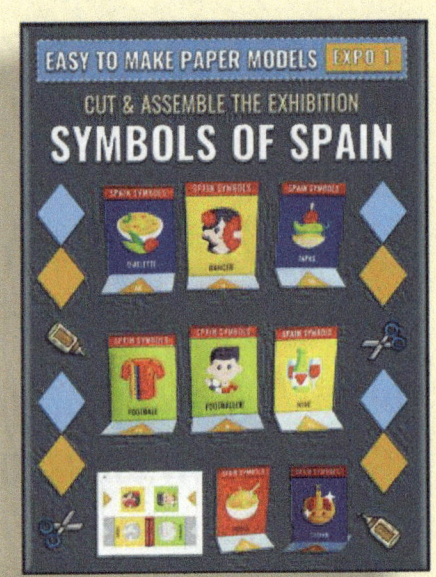

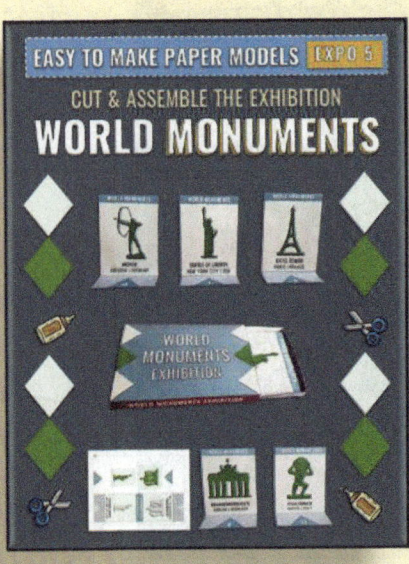

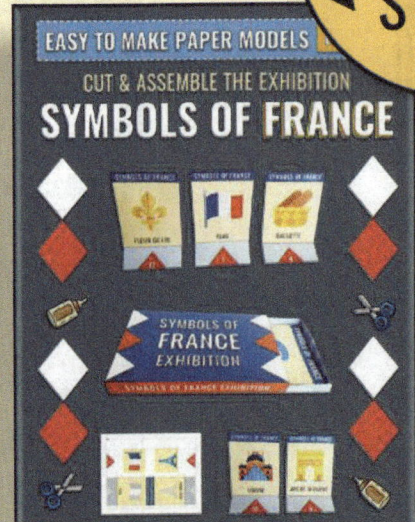

EASY TO STORE

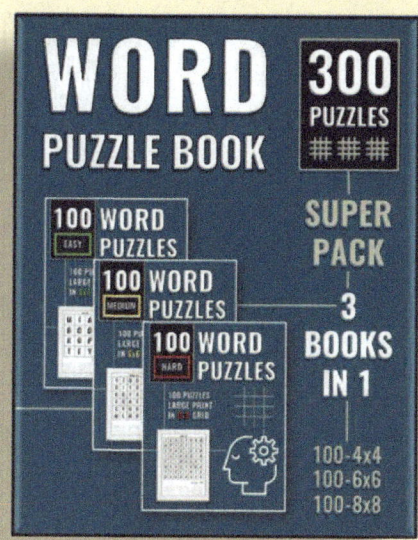

WORD PUZZLE BOOK

300 PUZZLES

100 WORD PUZZLES EASY

100 WORD PUZZLES MEDIUM

100 WORD PUZZLES HARD

SUPER PACK

3 BOOKS IN 1

100-4x4
100-6x6
100-8x8

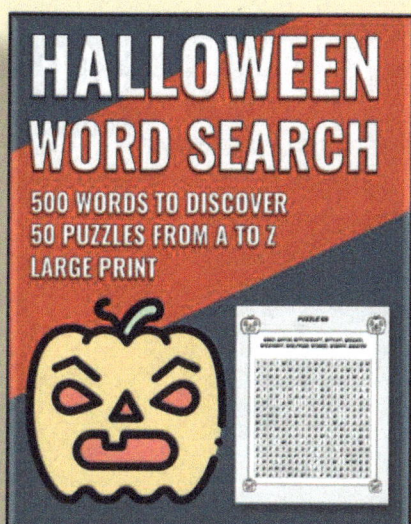

HALLOWEEN WORD SEARCH

500 WORDS TO DISCOVER
50 PUZZLES FROM A TO Z
LARGE PRINT

HAPPY WORD SEARCH

660 Positive Words to Discover, A to Z, Large Print

Think Positive Doing Search Puzzles

Be Calmer And Feel Happier

CHRISTMAS WORD SEARCH

MORE 500 WORDS TO DISCOVER
50 PUZZLES FROM A TO Z
IN LARGE PRINT

WORD SEARCH FOR DOG LOVERS

500 DOG NAMES TO DISCOVER
50 PUZZLES, IN LARGE PRINT, A TO Z
250 FEMALE NAMES, 250 MALES NAMES

Luna   Simba   Max
Molly   Mimi
Lulu   Duke
Dog   Theo

WORD SEARCH FOR CAT LOVERS

500 TOP CAT NAMES TO DISCOVER
50 PUZZLES, IN LARGE PRINT, A TO Z
250 FEMALE NAMES, 250 MALES NAMES

Kitty   Luna   Bella   Max
Tessa
Angel

GIRL NAMES WORD SEARCH

1.000 POPULAR NAMES TO DISCOVER
100 PUZZLES FROM A TO Z
LARGE PRINT

BOY NAMES WORD SEARCH

1.000 POPULAR NAMES TO DISCOVER
100 PUZZLES FROM A TO Z
LARGE PRINT

SOPA de LETRAS EN ESPAÑOL

75 ROMPECABEZAS CON LETRA GRANDE
750 PALABRAS NUEVAS EN ESPAÑOL

2 VOLUME

CALCUDOKU PUZZLE **500**
BOOK FOR ADULTS
PUZZLES
SUPER PACK
3 BOOKS IN 1
CALCUDOKU PUZZLE BOOK FOR 200
CALCUDOKU PUZZLE BOOK FOR 150
CALCUDOKU PUZZLE BOOK FOR ADULTS 150
200 4x4
150 6x6
150 9x9

MAZE **300 PUZZLES**
PUZZLE BOOK FOR ADULTS AND TEENS
SUPER PACK
3 BOOKS IN 1
MAZE 100
MAZE 100 M
MAZE 100 HARD
100-EASY
100-MEDIUM
100-HARD

HITORI **600 PUZZLES**
PUZZLE BOOK
★★★
SUPER PACK
3 BOOKS IN 1
HITORI PUZZLE BOOK 200 IN 4X4
HITORI PUZZLE BOOK 200 IN 7X7
HITORI PUZZLE BOOK 200 IN 9X9 GRID
200-4x4
200-7x7
200-9X9

SUDOKU **600 PUZZLES**
FOR KIDS 8-12
SUPER PACK
3 BOOKS IN 1
200 SUDOKU FOR KIDS 8-12
200 SUDOKU FOR KIDS 8-12
200 SUDOKU FOR KIDS 8-12
200 4x4
200 6x6
200 9x9

SUDOKU MONSTER
100 EASY SUDOKU
ONE PUZZLE PER PAGE
WITH SOLUTIONS
IN LARGE PRINT
SUDOKU MONSTER

WORD SEARCH MONSTER
50 WORD SEARCH PUZZLES
500+ SCARY WORDS TO DISCOVER
1 PUZZLE PER PAGE
WITH SOLUTIONS
IN LARGE PRINT
2
WORD SEARCH MONSTER

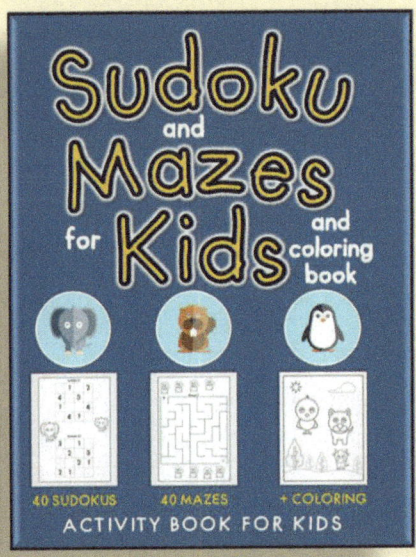

Sudoku and Mazes for Kids and coloring book
40 SUDOKUS
40 MAZES
+ COLORING
ACTIVITY BOOK FOR KIDS

500 **123 PATH**
PUZZLE BOOK
SUPER PACK 2 BOOKS IN 1
Volume 1 + Volume 2
250 123 PATH PUZZLE BOOK
250 123 PATH PUZZLE BOOK

500 **ABC PATH**
PUZZLE BOOK
SUPER PACK 2 BOOKS IN 1
Volume 1 + Volume 2
250 ABC PATH PUZZLE BOOK
250 ABC PATH PUZZLE BOOK